Angel's Diary

Martin Napa

Balboa Press books may be ordered through booksellers or by contacting:

Balboa Press
A Division of Hay House
1663 Liberty Drive
Bloomington, IN 47403
www.balboapress.com
844-682-1282

Because of the dynamic nature of the Internet, any web addresses or links contained in this book may have changed since publication and may no longer be valid. The views expressed in this work are solely those of the author and do not necessarily reflect the views of the publisher, and the publisher hereby disclaims any responsibility for them.

Any people depicted in stock imagery provided by Getty Images are models, and such images are being used for illustrative purposes only. Certain stock imagery © Getty Images.

ISBN: 978-1-9822-5349-3 (sc)
ISBN: 978-1-9822-5350-9 (e)

Library of Congress Control Number: 2020916023

Print information available on the last page.

Balboa Press rev. date: 09/17/2020

BALBOA.PRESS
A DIVISION OF HAY HOUSE

You feel a gentle touch on your shoulder. Surprised, you try to locate its source. You see no one. Still you feel that you're not alone. You look around and nearly stop your activities. Later, you might even forget that moment. But I surround you with love, and I am grateful that you noticed me.

The days, weeks, and our lives pass by. Yet I guide you through different times, lives, and places where you might linger. Through good, bad, and whatever you yourself have come to learn in this world, I will never leave you. I am your guardian angel.

I don't know if you'll read these lines now or after the passing of many years, in this life or in the next, or ever, but my love for you is endless. It is as endless as light is itself because love and light are one. I am thankful that I have been given the opportunity to send love in this way to you, to those who are close to you, and to all people because within love, we are all as one.

When you read this, you might wonder who or what these guardian angels are. Knowledge develops and matures within you as you go through different times. Because of your circumstances, talk of guardian angels may be foreign to you. Human beings have started to forget their guardian angels. There are many causes. You don't have to tire yourself with thoughts that may estrange you even further from me. Throughout time, there has been a veil of earthly knowledge between us. It is enough that you have lightly brushed it away. Now angels will appear before you. Angels are the ambassadors of God's love. They protect people with love. They awaken love in people.

But you don't have to think about any of this because love isn't born from thoughts. Love is born from feelings. Feelings are the eternal flame of love. Remember the most beautiful moments that you have felt. Remember the sensation that you felt at those moments. Acknowledge that sensation. Feel it again. Stay in that sensation. I can see how you fill yourself and your surroundings with love. It is like a glittering sun. You have created it yourself. Breathe it in. Breathe it in so deeply that the sensation reaches every nerve ending and cell in your body. I see that the all-embracing love is in you. You have become love.

If only that sensation would last forever, you have probably thought that many times. You have sometimes doubted that it could last very long. I have always been beside you, through everything that life has thrown at you and that has made you forget that feeling.

Actually, you don't need to remember those moments. Let them go into love. You will feel a lightness in yourself because you have freed yourself from them. Acknowledge your freedom because you were born free. You were born in love and of love. Love is free. The moment you think that the love you have experienced belongs to *you* is the moment you have imprisoned it.

Love cannot be measured or be weighed. The limitless cannot be limited. You chose your body when you came into this world, and your soul became one with your body. The soul thinks that because the body has limits, the love that belongs to the body should also have limits. Limitation breaks the flow of love, but the flow only breaks inside the body.

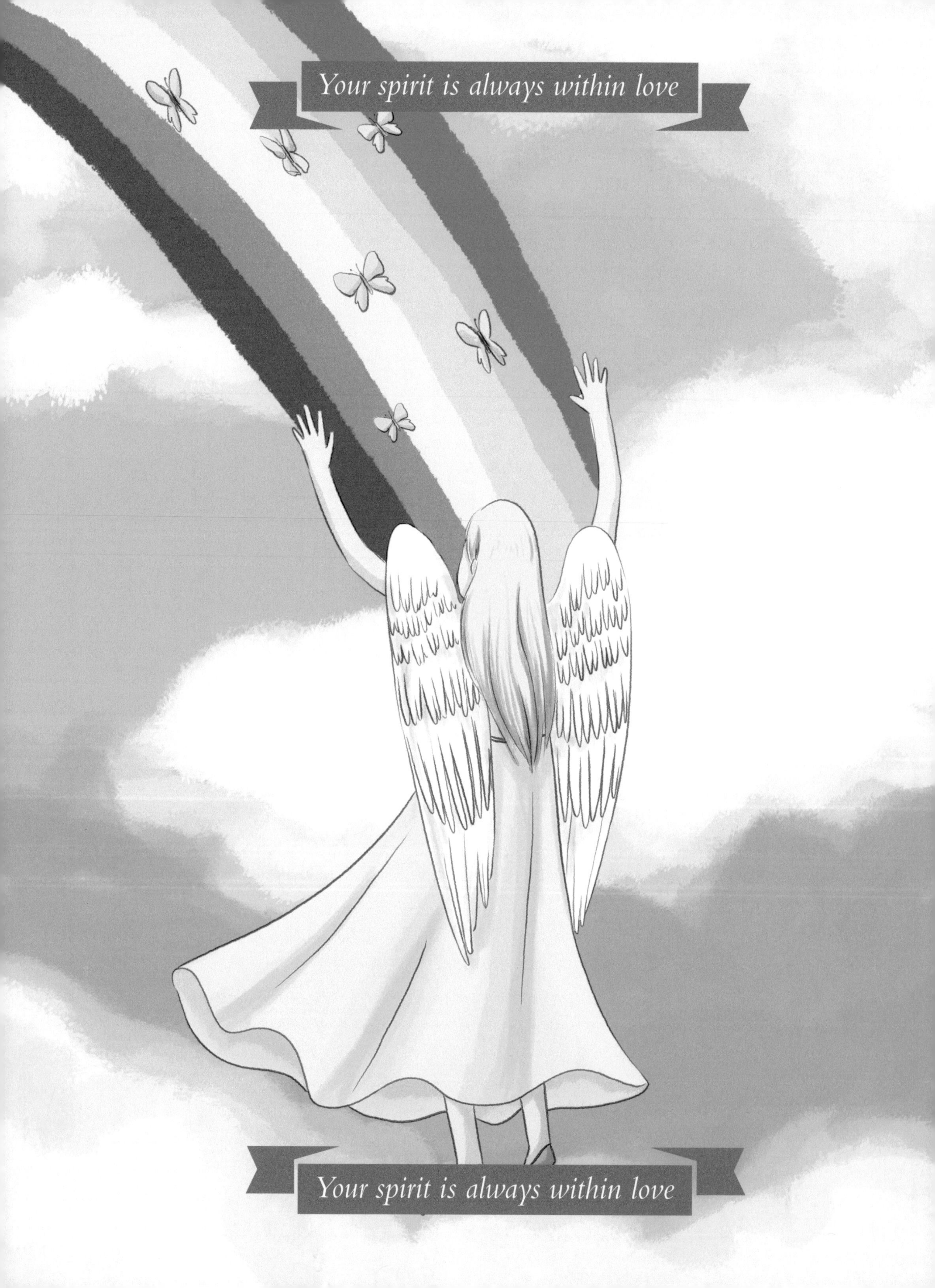

You have lived so many lives with the knowledge that who you are is your body and that your sacred spirit belongs to God. You have been imprisoned in your body, and your body has had to carry this heavy burden throughout time. Send love to your body and cherish it but remember that you are not the body but the spirit that chose your body, in this life, here and now.

I see that you hesitate slightly at this thought. Thoughts arise from your confusion, which needs to be limited. Feelings cannot be limited. Acknowledge the limitless and sense your contact with the universe. The universe is a spirit, and you are a part of that. But care for and respect the body that you have chosen for this life. The experiences you gain in this body will guide you on your journey.

I send you love. This is a loving opportunity to use my written words to tell you of my presence. Reading and understanding these written words won't change my continual place beside you. The words that you now read are simply a chance to help make sense of your wider range of feelings. A person's feelings always want to be supported by thoughts. The physical being also craves to be supported by thoughts. Use these words as an aid.

Every time you can't understand something that you have read, simply acknowledge it. Acknowledgment doesn't recognize limits, although this text was formed into this shape. I send love and thanks to all of those who helped place this text into your hands.

Your birth was not determined by chance. People consider moments, which they and their lives have so long awaited and prepared for, as happening by chance. Chance is a limitation, which a person's thoughts will not dare to cross. You consider the beginning of your as happening by chance because it is difficult to grasp the idea with your mind. Feelings always respond to chance.

You may believe that chance is an indiscriminate tool of fate. You're immediately ready to ask what your fate or destiny is. Destiny is movement. A person's destiny is a person's movement. Does the person move, or is it simply the fickle finger of fate? People have asked this throughout the ages.

For a moment, acknowledge love and breathe it in deeply. You need this now. In the word *fate*, the energy from previous, painful life experiences has approached you. Calmly breathe in love and stay in the feeling of love. Look at your beautiful hands and admire your fingers. These are your fingers of fate. Believe that sometimes the heavenly plan is to follow this direction your fingers are pointing at.

I send you love.

Accept this love.

Accept being within love.

Your spirit remembers your previous lives' experiences. These are difficult to free yourself from. You have tried to liberate yourself from them. I can see your efforts. You believe that you don't need to recollect them, but you sometimes feel that it is difficult to escape those memories. You have acknowledged that this is part of you, and you can't help that. Breathe in love. Breathe again.

Only the burden in your heart restrains you from rising into life's lightness. Sometimes, the guilt you have inherited from previous ages won't allow you to be within love. Whether your choice is to continue to live with the burden of your past life and to look longingly at love from the outside or to finally become that love yourself?

Would you like me to help you free yourself from all that restrains you from moving on? Would you like to hear and see the story of your lives through the eyes of love? That story will change into love, and once more, you will feel yourself as love. Love liberates. The feeling of love is everlasting because that is part of love's existence. Acknowledge that you are ready for this, but you can only do this through love. People need to accept the past and the present through love. Only then is it possible to move on. Moving on is a chance for life.

I send you love.

Accept this love.

Accept being within love.

Often, when you come from swimming or bathing, you quickly grab a towel to warm yourself. I always send you love. I hope that you will sometimes remember that moment when you came from your mother's womb into this world. That was your first shock, which to this day, you haven't quite recovered from. It was the cold sensation that greeted you outside of your mother's warmth. Every time you emerge from water, that memory returns.

Remember that first moment and acknowledge it. Send love to that moment and stay within that love. In this way, you began your miraculous journey through life. That is when you had your first experience, so bless it. In this way, bless all your previous lives and the one that follow with love and forgiveness. You are within love.

Look again at your moment of birth and see the miracle. This moment is also when you meet yourself, here and now, in this life.

I send you love.

Accept this love.

Accept being within love.

Now be aware of the times when you are swimming or bathing. How refreshing that sensation is. Don't immediately grab a towel but cherish the moment, as every cell in your body fills with the lightness of love. It's that simple.

Although beliefs have differed over time, the natural understanding of the childbirth helps to nurture the close bond between the mother and a child. This postnatal contact with the mother—when the baby is gently placed on the mother's breast—is a feeling that gives reassurance for a lifetime. But there have been times when the baby has been separated from the mother after birth. You have experienced this yourself. I see how the weight of this isolation approaches you.

Breathe in love.

I send you overwhelming love. Calmly breathe it in and stay within it. People have believed different things. You have experienced other lives. Breathe in deeply. You are now within love's protection. The moment that you are aware of my presence, you can always call me—always. I am beside you—always. The flow of love into you and through you will never cease.

Look back at that moment after your birth, when you were in a room with other babies. At that moment, your only feeling was a longing for your mother. Send love into those moments. Send love to everyone who was in that room. Believe that in that same moment no matter where they are in the world now, things suddenly became lighter for them. We are all one through love.

Look even further back into the depths of your memory to when you were born through pain and guilt. Send love to your mother. In those moments, she also saw the world through the veil of her own ordeal. She has had to feel it for herself as well as on your behalf. That has been the cause of her pain. Send love to your mother and accept the lightness that comes when the flood of love washes you both. Breathe in that lightness and be within it with your mother. Feel how every mother in this world, who is connected through this painful experience, begins to feel lighter. Love feels no limits. The message of love reaches everyone.

Acknowledge your love.

Acknowledge being within love.

Be in it.

Be in it with your mother.

Be in it with all mothers.

Be within love, with everyone, always.

Pain from those distant moments that united you with your mother has left and changed into love. The lightness of love has united you again. Love is everything.

Feel the moment and let your thoughts roam free. Try to feel if there is any more heaviness in your heart, which won't allow you to stay in everlasting love. Is there something else? Feelings don't lie, but you try to deny them. Those thoughts are too difficult to feel, and that difficulty won't release you. You know that you don't need those thoughts.

Keep your eyes and your heart open. Only through love and being within love can you return to those feelings you experienced, when your mother decided to abandon you. Stay within love. I will always protect you. Take a deep breath. You can do that solely within love.

Within love

Within love

Within love

That was your mother's choice. You also made a choice to stay within your mother and not to be born into this world. Forgive your mother and forgive yourself. You chose those circumstances together with your mother. You both made the decision to choose that path. You both made that choice. It was your joint decision. Recognize how love formed a bridge across the chasm between you. Now you are one again. You are together. You don't have to hold back your tears because tears are the pearls in the necklace of life's experiences. They guide you to recognize love.

I send you love.

Accept this love.

Accept being within love.

Love is everywhere, both within you and around you. The thought of the loving relationship between you and your mother and being with her within this love is the most important memory to take with you when you step into life's journey. Always begin your journey with love. Then your journey will be blessed with love.

If you haven't done this yet, you can always begin your journey again. The journey is never permanently finished, and you can always return to the beginning. Only your understanding holds you back. Breathe in love. Stay in it. Worldly limitations are created from people's thoughts and knowledge. You are always free. This sensation of freedom allows you to move freely back and forth in time.

What ties you to the past? Feeling does, of course. But love is feeling. Filling the past with love creates a new feeling toward the past. Everything that is not of love clings to the past. Everything that is of love frees you to enter into love permanently and eternally. The past, the present, and the future are missing in love's permanence. Love frees you from today's limits because love doesn't have limits.

Your past, which is fiction, is merely the collection of thoughts that you remember about the past. As long as we think about the past, the past has a hold on us. As soon as we acknowledge the past, we receive help from the feeling of love. Love without limits will fill the past, the present, and the future. The past, the present, and the future will become one with love in this way—one whole. You will also become whole.

Around you, I see a distracting sadness, which is trying to stay close to you. Send love into it. Thoughts distract you. You think that even though you yearned for love, your mother didn't answer that yearning with the same kind of love. Throughout their lives, perhaps people have thought that the love they received was always less than they had given. Now I see that same sadness clinging to the mother, and it won't let go because she also thinks that she hasn't received as much love as she has given.

I send you love.

Acknowledge your love.

Accept being within love.

Breathe deeply of it.

Be in it.

Cast your loving glance at life and other lives. You have experienced these feelings of sadness and loneliness. At those moments, you have somehow felt cut off. What are you cut off from? Love! A person starts measuring love at those moments. To measure love, one has to set limits on love. But how do you limit the limitless? The limitless cannot be limited. Love cannot be measured.

How much have you shared? How much have others shared with you? When you open yourself, love flows into you, and you see that the flow of love has no limits. Send love into those moments, and those moments will be filled with love. Look how also those together with you who used to measure love are miraculously filled with love. Look! Those past moments are all filled with love, and the past becomes part of the wholesome present. Everything is filled with love. There is enough love for everyone forever. One person does not have an advantage over another regarding receiving greater love. All are equal.

A person tends to create a gap, opening or channel through which to connect with the flow of love. But why do some look at love through a small gap while others bathe in love's flow? That depends on the extent that the person has pushed the veil of earthly illusions away.

Sometimes take a closer look at a person who is glowing with love. There are people who have never had such a veil of separation in front of them. But neither is better than the other. One of them has had more worldly experiences than the other one has, but everyone has had the same opportunity to be within love.

Acknowledge your love.

Acknowledge love without limits and inhale it.

I notice that you can't quite release your thoughts about those who are radiant with love. You also want to be like that, but for some reason, you think that you can't. You feel envy and somehow deprived. Send love into that feeling. You have a human body, so understand those feelings through love. You don't have to feel guilty about your envy. Your whole life within you and around you is just as it is. Accept it naturally. It will provide an opportunity to see everything through love.

Humans are accustomed to comparing themselves with others and to appraising them. This is a human foible, and denying it merely adds to it. The result of denial is merely to enlarge it. Release from denial provides an opportunity to escape from all that is a result of denial and not of love.

Breathe in deeply of love.

You are love.

You send love everywhere.

I see how love flows through you. Isn't it a wonderful sensation? Be in it. Simply be. You now think of those moments when you have simply wanted to be. Tiredness from continual rushing has made you simply want to be, even for a moment. To simply be means that love flows through you, and you yourself are love. It's that simple.

You may not yet feel that one energy has come closer to you. It is near you and in you. Soon you may feel it. You started thinking about something, as if you wanted to catch some feeling from it that you can't quite put into words. This is how it all happens. Accept it.

You focused on your mother … true. Suddenly, you thought about your father. Why? It is because his energy came closer to you. You were born of your mother and your father on this earth. You came from your mother and your father. Acknowledge how this pair of words strikes a balance in your feelings. Send love to all those feelings that relate to your mother or your father.

I send you love.

You are within love.

This is not merely a question of balancing your mother's and father's energy. It is also a question of your balance. It is also a question of the world's balance and that of the universe's.

Send love to your father. He needs it as much as your mother does. So often, tedious traditions have separated children and fathers. Send love to your father, to his loneliness, and to the resultant guilt, and you will create a miracle. Loneliness and guilt are a heavy inheritance, which is passed from father to son and in turn, to the next generation of sons. The inherited responsibility of fathers to protect their homes has kept them close to home but not within the home. They haven't been able to be within, although in their hearts, this is what they may have wanted.

Send love into those feelings, and you will release that inheritance so that your father may reach home. He is part of your home.

I send you love.

You are wonderful love.

Let love flow through your mother, father, and you. Acknowledge how love releases the stress in your mother and father, which started on the day when they learned that you were to be born. The veil of history has tied birth to pain, tension, and responsibility. This has stifled a natural relationship with the child.

A child is a miracle, belonging both to the father and to the mother. A child is a natural miracle, and one born of love that creates love. A child is never an accident, incidental, a one-night stand's small mistake, or some other occasion that burdens a person with guilt. You know that chance is God's tool of destiny. At just that moment, just those two people, in just that way created the miracle that brought you into this world. Send wonderful love into that moment, and everything that follows will carry you through love.

You are love.

Send love to your mother and to your father. Be with them within love.

Your mother and father have waited a long time for this moment, and now they can be part of this love at last. I see how their love doesn't cease, but also flows back to their mother and father. Love fills every part of us, which we have inherited from our ancestors.

That is love.

I see your thoughts. I know where you stopped, hesitated, and wondered if you were understood. I see you looking at the past and at your mother and father. Their hesitation and fear hold you now. But you know what to do. You are love. Send that into every feeling that your mother and father have ever felt. All that wasn't love will become love because love has no limits. Can you feel how light you have suddenly become? Breathe in that lightness and be that lightness because love is lightness.

You are love.

Your mother is love.

Your father is love.

You, your mother, and your father are love.

You, your mother, and your father are love.

I see how these words strengthen your love and lift you into the lightness of being. The feelings and thoughts that have held you back have been released into love. Therefore, everything will become love. That is the miracle of love. Love is a miracle.

Do you suddenly feel more miracles beside you? Of course, you do. The energy from your sisters and brothers has found you. The energy and power of your mother's, father's, and your love are so great that all your family members feel it, wherever they are in the past, the present, or the future. You all became one in this instant. You are a holy family. That is miraculous.

But acknowledge it further. You certainly feel. Your sisters and brothers arrived immediately at the call of love, but give them a moment and take a moment yourself. Send love to your sisters and brothers, and you will suddenly feel how love flows back toward you. It is so necessary that sisters and brothers fill their relationships with love because their inherited understanding has made them want to compete for the love of the mother and the father.

Release yourself from all thoughts and recollections of past events that occurred between you and your sisters and brothers, as a result of competing for the love of your mother or father. Love has no limits. One cannot be loved more and the other less. One can only be loved.

Breathe love in deeply and be in it.

Everything that was needs to be filled with love.

Do it now.

Love.

Everything else turns into love.

Take your time and breathe in peacefully. Relationships with brothers and sisters are vital on this earth and in this life because your inherited closeness through your parents forms a powerful bond of energy between you. The completion for this energy through love is the only way you can move on. Come together with your brothers and sisters. Create your own circle. You need it now. Let love fill this circle and feel it. Together, acknowledge how love flows, fulfilling everyone and everything, without knowing any limits. There is only love.

Now, love is everywhere. Go to your mother and father and place them in the middle of your circle. Acknowledge the lightness that fills your mother and father. Finally, they are in the middle of the circle. Throughout time, your mother and father have pictured only one thing: the child or children that are in between them. They are busy as they move around the child or children. They revolve around the children, with the mother on one side and the father on the other because children need protection around them all the time. So, they twirl around the children never being in the center themselves, barely meeting each other.

Send love there.

Love.

Love.

Let the parents now be at the center. Feel, how their hearts are filled with peace. Look how love brings back lightness and makes them radiant again. So, parents no longer need to be at the center of the circle. They take each other by the hand, and a moment later, they

embrace. The powerful flow of love floods through their being. They move back and take the hands of their children. A united family circle is formed. You all move together holding hands. An endless love flows in this sacred family circle. That is love.

Be within love.

Always.

Look at this wonderful scene. It is real. Look, how your mother's mother and father are joining your mother. See, how your father's mother and father are joining him too. And now, the sisters and brothers of your mother and father move into this wonderful circle as well. First of all, they go to the center of the circle to cleanse themselves with love from everything that is not love. Look at how after this miraculous cleansing, they approach those in the circle, and the circle grows bigger.

The circle of love is ever expanding.

Look at how even more people come into the circle and the previous confines disappear. You soon see that the circle has become so large that it is impossible to count all the people inside of it. But you don't need to count them. You can't measure love. You can feel love. Accept being within love and be in it. You are within love, and everything around you is love.

Give up looking for logic, as this is happening because there is no thought process behind it. What is happening is free of thought because thought is unnecessary here. Accept this. Most of the things in this world, which happen without thought, remain longer than those that result from thought because thought sets limits, and limits are only there to be overcome. This way, the limits set by thought become limitless freedom, and freedom is love.

Therefore, you don't need to allow thought to restrain the dream that tries to appear before you. Bravely see how the radiant circle of love continues to grow without limits until it surrounds the whole world. This beautiful circle embraces the entire world with love. That is really happening now. It truly is because the world you were born into yearns to be in it.

Acknowledge it with your entire loving self. The power of love fills the earth because it too, can now be in the center of the circle of love at last. But love has no limits, and everything is filled with love—everything. Everything becomes love—everything—even that which is not love.

I wish you could see your world from a distance. The brightness of love is mighty, and that love moves as a mighty river into the wide universe. Our message to the universe is the message of love. You are marvelous in this love. Be in it and breathe it in. Hold that feeling forever. Everything that happens is marvelous. It is real. It is reality.

Love.

Love.

Love.

And nothing more is needed. Breathe in calmly. Stay in it. Stay in it even more. You need this now because I can see how the mortal memories of the past are trying to cling to you. But

send them love. This is an opportunity to stay within love. This is the escape route from the clinging memories of the past because human memory is filled with this clinging emotion.

Humanity has had to cling to life and food. Sometimes humanity has thought it necessary to cling to someone else's life. Humanity needs love to become free from the pummeling of memories. Simply send love there. Let the flow of love be steady. One can be certain that quite soon the painful lump of memory will be dissolved into love. Look closely at how that happens and be assured because love is supreme. One only has to let love into oneself and the world.

Acknowledge how love fills every fiber in your body. Accept it. How marvelous that feeling is. Everything is filled with love once more. You shine. You are within love. You are marvelous. To be so, you need nothing more than to open yourself to love. I see how you wallow in love's flow. Yes. Be amazed and acknowledge it. You are radiant.

You are love.

You are love. We are love.

We are love.

Everything is love.

Everything is love.

Be in this because this is everything, and everyone needs this. Without this, everything is lost. The reason why not everything is lost is because love is the beginning of everything, and everything eventually reaches love. That is how everyone becomes love.

I see how the words "everything is not lost" touched you with painful thoughts. You might be wondering where these thoughts come from if everything is within love. You needed this moment right now. This was an opportunity to understand, through love, what is not of love. To understand is to stay within love and to give love. This is the purpose of this moment. This timely moment is to allow a change into love. In this time, love is born.

But wars, starvation, poverty, despair, sickness, hostility, hatred, death, oppression, treason, and deprivation scream deficiency – no more words are needed here because each word prompts a memory that screams a deficiency of love. Every memory evokes pain because each of these words call for love and hold a reminder of that which is not of love. Where do painful memories come from? Why are they here if everything is love? They come from thoughts and the current understanding that there is not enough of everything. They come from humanity's thinking that a person is a body and not a spiritual being. Wars start from thinking that there is not enough of something and that some are better than others are. Using these excuses, they look for ways to destroy bodies. But after the bodies are destroyed, souls remain, screaming for light.

If people could only see with their own eyes that on the battlefields, the lost souls call for light, even to this day. Send them light. You are from the light. Help your soul and send everyone who seeks it into the light. It would be easier to live in the world, and the world would become lighter. The world would receive love and be within love.

You are within love's protective shield.

You are love.

You yourself share love with everyone who seeks it because love never ends.

There is enough love for everyone who asks for it because love is all.

Take a deep breath. You are love. You are love even when you hear words that are not of love but call out for love. Stay within love when you hear of war. Send love to everyone who is in that war. Breathe in and see how the people around you also breathe in. Love. Breathe together. Love. Everything that you breathe out, breathe into love. Send love into wars and into those who develop wars, and the creation of wars will cease because love fills everything.

Love is in everyone and everything.

It only has to be awakened in everything because everything is of love, and love is everything.

Now surround the words *starvation*, *poverty*, and *despair* with love. Send love to those words—love without limits and light. People have created these words. They are created from the illusion that speaks of starvation, poverty, and despair. Starvation, poverty, and despair do not exist. I see how you are filled with surprise and wonder how it could be so. Doubt holds you within the world that you long to be freed from.

Breathe love in and know that your thoughts create that world in which you live. Thought is the source of this life. Thoughts of shortage create shortage. Thoughts of abundance create abundance. That is how the people in this world have chosen to experience that illusion.

Be within love, and love will give the answers to all. Pour love and light along with playful joy into all the illnesses in the world and into those illnesses that have previously filled you with fear. Admire the way in which all the illnesses of the world free themselves through the flow of love and light and change into love and light. Illness is humanity's codependence, in its own illusion that there is not enough love and that it has to struggle in this lack of love.

There is never a lack of love. Humanity is love after all. If there were no love, there wouldn't be humans. Love has no limits. Humanity's way into love is similarly without limitation. Illness is merely a reminder for the doubters. Send love to all the doubters in the world and shower them with the sparkling rain of love and light. You can do it because you are light and love. Admire how love and light fill everything.

Everything is love.

The enmity between people also calls out for love because people are tired of hatred. Take the enmity tenderly into your arms and rock it in love's cradle. After all, enmity arises in those who were born into this world and were not held tenderly to feel love's embrace. Send love to all of those people in the world, take them tenderly into your arms, and embrace them in love's cradle. You know how. You will see how all those people will be freed from the illusion that they are not loved enough.

There is never a shortage of love for anyone because love is all. Wonder at how all those people slide into a sweet dream while in your embrace. Listen to how peacefully they breathe.

Listen to how they breathe as one. They are all love's children. Look at how the miserable enmity and hatred, which you took into your embrace, have changed into love.

Dormant in people's hearts, the embrace has awakened into beautiful love. It's that simple. Awaken the world into love. Rock these beloved people in your arms and plant mother's tenderness and father's warmth around them. After all, they are all love. Gently lay these people into rainbow hammocks, which are tied with golden ropes between apple trees that reach to the sky. Let them drowse in these heavenly hues because when they awake, they too will look at the world in different colors. They too will understand what it once meant to taste the first apple from the apple tree.

We are of love.

We are love.

No one has ever betrayed anyone. People have never betrayed anyone. People can finally stop feeling distressed over the world's deceit. Send love to all of those who struggle over the illusion of distress. They think that they are deceitful or that other people think that of them. Love allows us to forget the word *deceit* because everything becomes love.

Even deceit turns into love.

Be within love.

Surround yourself with eternal light. Be within eternal love.

Everything is born of love. Everything becomes love. It is the same with the deceiver, which people call death. Send love to all those thoughts and feelings about death, which you have thought or felt in the past. Breathe in love. Be within love. Fill the word *death* with love because everything is love. Free the pain of loss into love. Everything fills with love.

People don't fear a beautiful bridge that crosses one flower-bedecked bank to another in a lush, leafy green park. They move eagerly across the bridge toward new, wonderful discoveries. The same is true of the bridge that people refer to as death. It is merely a connection between love's limitless fields. It is only a connection from love into love with love's power.

Anyone who has decided to turn back from that bridge speaks often of the angels who welcomed that person with love and with care. Angels are always with people, even at the most difficult times. Angels are love and so are people.

Everything is love.

Everything is light.

Love is light.

Light is love.

Love.

Light

Love.

Breathe in deeply and fill all your rambling thoughts with love. These thoughts arise when you read these lines. Perhaps you didn't even notice this. Let everything become love. Get

used to being within eternal love and filling all your thoughts, no matter what kind they may be, always with love. Then you will always be within love.

Everything is love.

Everything is light.

Love is light.

Light is love.

Love.

Light

Love.

Breathe in peacefully and try to relax. Try not to think of anything. Breathe in and out several times. Of course, love. As you read these lines, try not to think about anything. For a moment, take a look behind you and see in your mind's eye what a broad fan of thoughts and feelings you have created while you were reading these lines. These feelings and thoughts are yours, especially those that you weren't even conscious of while you were reading.

Look at that fan. Look at it with love and send love to your beloved fan. These thoughts and feelings were in the memory chest of your previous lives, and they started to stretch when you touched them. But you don't have to measure the size and weight of your fan. Stroke your fan with the brush of golden love and send love to those thoughts and feelings. They have waited a long time for this. They need this now. You have awakened them. Now send them into love.

When people's curiosity takes them back into the thoughts and feelings of the past, it may startle them, and they might forget to view all these past experiences through a loving look. Then the past may become the present. Fill and surround yourself with love, now and always. Those moments need love, people need love, curiosity needs loving understanding, and all past thoughts and feelings need love. Then the past can become love. Becoming love is no longer important to the past, the present, and the future because love is now, everywhere, and forever.

Look and admire how your beautiful fan glitters with golden sparks at every stroke of your brush. Look and admire how those golden sparks of light cover your fan. Soon you'll see the gleam of a fabulous golden light. Your fan has become a golden light, which spreads love everywhere because that is the reason why we are here and that is what we experience. A golden light, which is bright with love, is born in everything.

I see how the words that you have read and the thoughts and feelings that you have experienced ask to be alone with you. Acknowledge this. Pause, relax, and let your spirit guide you. You don't have to do anything. Just let yourself be. This also makes it easier for your spirit. If you feel that you need to, close the book and open it again when you feel your spirit directing you to do so. I love you—always. We are within love—always.

You are within light.

You are light.

You are remarkable, and remarkable feelings radiate from you. I thank you for starting to read these lines. I love you always. Angels love you always. God loves you always. Feel and acknowledge this always.

I noticed a quiver in your spirit when you read the word *God*. That quiver broke the flow of love for a moment. The word *God* has been imposed upon people's consciousness throughout time, many times not in love. Because of that, many have given up following the word of God. Many things have been done in the name of God that were not loving. Many times, something has been called God that was not God.

Painful, earthly memories have lowered an earthly veil between God and humanity. Some people have used this and have started to establish themselves as the intermediary between those behind the veil and God. But all these eras have never survived.

Send love to all of those intermediaries. You know that you can do it because the flow of love cannot be measured. Send love there because they have been waiting for it for a long time. Free them into love. They need love. They need the feeling of love because love is a feeling.

One can know God and not speak about it, but one should certainly feel, because God is the feeling of love. After all, God is eternal love. Breathe in love and you breathe in God. Be within love and you are within God. Be love and you are a child of God. Then you are one with God.

Imagine yourself in the middle of a field of flowers. Forget yourself as you are in the heavenly beauty of flowers and breathe in the freshness and the spirit of life around you. Imagine magical worlds in the dewdrops, which are sparkling in the sunshine. Cast your eyes on the blue heavens and listen to the birdsong, which glorifies love. All of this is the greatest reality because everything is God. All of that is love.

It is within your power to make and create all of that. If you don't notice it around you immediately, close your eyes and observe how your mind's eye becomes enthusiastic again for those fields of love. At some moment, recognize this. Open your eyes, and it all comes to light.

You are of the Creator.

You are the Creator.

You are of love.

You are love.

You create love.

Look at a child who runs and skips around a field of flowers without a care. Look and admire the child's lightness and happiness. Look carefully and follow every movement. You see how joyfully the child's arms circle about. The child is happily hopping from one leg to the other, bending to the flowers, and trying to innocently play with the butterflies that rise from the flowers. Look. That is you. As long as you recognize yourself there, you are within love. For this time, you exist for yourself, here and now.

Here and now.

Within love.

Look at your hands. Marvel at your fingers. Place your open palms side by side as if you are catching an abundance of light falling from heaven. Recognize the moment when the light that you have gathered in your hands needs to be lifted to your face. Pour the light onto your face and feel how pureness and freshness flows into every pore of your skin.

Leave your hands on your face for a moment so that your fingers are slightly above your eyebrows. After tenderly stroking your face, take your hands away. Do you feel something opening up? Repeat it again. Wash your face with the light of heavenly abundance. Wash your face with a feeling of love. Then open your hands. Can you feel a break of a new dawn. It only feels new. After all, you come from this world. It is yours. Do you remember this? This is the world of love, here, now, forever. If the humanity around you sometimes makes you doubt this, you know what to do: reach for the infinite heavenly light and wash your face with love so that your eyes can see what is there. It is love.

Listen to love. Lift the light that flows from love to your ears. Lovingly hold your ears and then take your hands away. Listen as eternal love sends you news of abundance. You are a witness to this because you hear love. You hear this sublime music. This is love.

Gather love into your hands and lift that wonderful light to your heart. Put your light-filled hands on your heart and lovingly hold them there. Feel how your heart fills with light. Feel how your heart fills with love. Feel how your heart is full of light and love. Your heart is full of light and love.

Light and love.
Love and light.
Light and love.
Love and light.

Go to a sunny beach. Take off your shoes and step into the warm sand. Feel how the sun-kissed sand lovingly caresses your feet. Walk into the sea and feel its water cooling your feet. Step back onto the sand and enjoy its warmth. Then let the cooling seawater refresh your feet again. Close your eyes and turn your face toward the sun. Listen to the sounds of the waves.

You are in the middle of perfection with your entire body, enjoy it, be in this perfection. Feel it. Let light embrace your body. Remember being a child running free on the beach. Let this golden light fill your body. You don't have to do anything for this. You don't have to strain yourself because light is everywhere. Let it flow into you. Feel this.

Feel your eternal contact with light. You are always in light. You are a child of the light. Believe it. Become a carrier of light. Just remember the light from which you came into this world. Just remember the light that filled you when you came into this world. Remember!

You might ask where that light has disappeared to during all these years. The light has not gone anywhere. It is always within and around you. It is just the same as your guardian angels are. They carry and keep the light when you get tired and forget the light.

Why do people forget light? Light is love, and love is light. When a person forgets light, love is also forgotten. It might be forgotten when a person is cut off from the flow of light and love. When a person starts to fear that he or she is alone, that person actually feels alone. Being alone stops a person from being in the flow of light and love. When a person fears he or she won't have enough strength and energy, that is how the individual will feel before long. The steady flow of love and light will be interrupted. This happens only in this human world. God's love and light are infinite but human fair will stop it flowing effortlessly. Thinking without feeling closes the flow of the person's energy, which is his or her connection with the wellspring of love and light. Feeling without thinking keeps a person in the flow but his or her contact with the reality of this world can fade out.

Accepting love gives you spiritual strength.

Knowing love gives you mental strength.

But everything originates from love and reaches love.

Love.

Love.

Love.

Do you recognize these words or sometimes think of them? Recognizing and repeating them sends you strength. The repetition of thinking them starts to annoy you. When the repetition no longer annoys you, you are released from your sea of thoughts and into the sunshine of love.

Awaken into the light that has led you here. Recognize that light. Fill and surround yourself with the light into which you were born. Again, begin the path that you started when you came into this world. Let your inner child of light guide you through your childhood and create the childhood you have dreamed of.

This is all reality because you have created it. Know that you take your mother's and father's loving blessings with you on that path and the caring truth of your brothers and sisters. You are not alone on that path, regardless of anything that tries to remind you of the loneliness you have felt through the years and have lived in the past. Now you walk along that path in the power of love and light.

Look again at those people you encountered outside your family's circle. Look again at your childhood playmates. Send all of them limitless love because no one that you meet on the path of life is there by chance. Everyone you meet has an important message to you so that you can continue your path and make the choices that will bring peace to your heart.

If any of those people in your childhood have hurt you and brought sorrow into your heart, forgive them. Forgiveness is the bridge to the everlasting flow of love. Forgiveness opens the door to freedom. People have closed this door because of their anger, sorrow, and despair. These feelings need to be released and sent into light.

Everything that is not of the light, actually, yearns for the light. The more light is denied, the greater the subconscious yearning for light becomes. That is why all those moments where there was a shortage of light now need light afresh. That is how darkness changes into light. Humankind doesn't need to fear the darkness because darkness disappears into the light.

Without rushing, look at those people who remind you of your childhood. Study them carefully. Observe their feelings and thoughts. Track what they have sent you through that contact. Was it love or something else?

Bless the love that they have sent, and you will see that their love fills them and you. Take part in that love. Send everything else into love, and you will see how it changes into love and light. Look again at all those people, and you will be convinced that there is nothing in them but love and that you will receive nothing from them but love. It's that simple. One needs only to love.

Go back to your childhood. Go into the dreamland of your immediate childhood. Most people on this earth have kept their ties with childhood through their dreams. Do you see your childhood as a distant black-and-white silent film that passes in front of your eyes in slow motion? Do you occasionally long for something distant and unattainable? Do you long for the sense of security that your distant childhood offered? Be in that land of your childhood and look around with that child's eyes.

Does something that you don't want to see suddenly appear before your eyes? Can you touch that painful moment in the slow motion of the silent film? Seek inside yourself and look.

Be within love.

Be always within love, whether through good or evil.

Evil has touched you because you will help it change to good. You will reach into light and into love.

When you see your childhood as a distant silent movie, you know that you have started to forget the child within you. When the moments that you don't want to remember suddenly

come close enough for you to touch, know that you have not let them go and that they continue to be with you.

Now you have the opportunity. Take it because you are a child of light forever. Go back into that silent movie together with the light. Reach into the stills of your childhood's silent movie and take a deep breath. Breathe in light and love from everything around you. Then breathe out love and light into the images of your childhood's silent movie. You will see a miracle.

The black-and-white film will start to take on colors. Yes, love's green will start to appear in the film shots. Rainbow hues will find their proper places on every little black-and-white segment. You will be convinced that the slow-moving stills of the silent movie are beginning to move faster. They suddenly come to life. They become faster and touchable.

Now comes the moment. From between your lips, release a loud sound that you love most of all. Open your mouth and listen to it. Listen how that silent movie now has the beautiful sounds of a passionate masterpiece, which you have created. It is no longer distant but right here. All is with you here and now. You can lose yourself in that wonderful film at any time because you no longer have to search or wait for it. It is all within you.

Do you still see those moments that you don't want to remember? Don't fear them because fear is the strongest affirmation of all that is not love. Look again at those moments. If you're going to swallow something, swallow only love and nothing else. Look at those moments and know that they were only there to help you understand what love was and what it was not. Know that those moments have come to you to ask for your help. With your strength and love, they can return to the love and the light that they have yearned for. Give them that opportunity.

Look at those moments with a childlike openness and tell yourself that this is right. When you have done so, you have given your consciousness a chance to release those moments and those feelings of love, which you send into those moments. You no longer have to struggle in the labyrinth of memory. Do it! Every person on this earth has the strength to do so. You are a child of light, and you will succeed through your wonderful lightness. You can do it. Look and marvel at how love fills everything.

Love fills everything.

Everything is filled with light.

Everything becomes love

Everything becomes love

Move further into the land of your childhood and again, reach out through all those childhood years that you can remember, the good as well as the bad. Don't dread that journey. Be happy that now you are free to look back at those years and that nothing will pressure or ruin you. You are free because you are a child of love and no one can hurt you again. Walk through those years with love.

Every child on this earth is born with the knowledge of love and light. But the touch of this world brings a sleeping draught of forgetfulness regarding love and light. You might ask why that sleeping draught is necessary. It was your choice to experience this, as is everyone's choice in the entire universe.

Look at it this way. You decided to come from light to bring light into this world. You did not come into this world to suffer. Acknowledge the difference between these two feelings and make your choice. Your decision is sacred, and the whole universe will protect it. The universe respects also those who have decided to shut their eyes for a moment, to suffer, so that when they open them again, they can feel a boundless welcome from all that are in light and love. It is that simple. Look at how easy it is to feel all that because senses have no limits.

Try to release that thought, and suddenly, you find yourself no longer at the dead end. You don't need those dead ends anymore. You need limitless freedom. You need eternal light. You need love. Know that angels are always with you, in everything you do, and everywhere you go. Just open your heart, and you will see and feel yourself within the protective circle of angels.

Look around you.

Look with your heart.

See yourself surrounded with a wonderful light.

That light gives you courage and a feeling of security. That light instills a belief in yourself and in others. That light gives you a limitless sense of freedom and oneness with everything—everything that is of light and love in the universe. Know that angels are with you.

Angels are givers. They bring light and love from wells that can never be empty. Remember your first contact with this world. Look back at yourself to when you shared your toys with other children. Remember those moments when you were a giver. Remember how you experienced joy in giving. Know that you have come into this world to give and to bring love and light.

But remember yourself in those moments when you started to take toys from the other children. You started to shove those children to get their toys or to protect your siblings from the others. Look at those moments and feel the sensation that you experienced caused by the fear of going without. The fear that you would be without something was a message to the universe that you wanted to experience the feeling of loss. The universe gave it to you.

But send that feeling away and experience love. Fill everything that happened through your choice with light. Tell yourself that you no longer need those experiences because you have felt and understood that love and light are everywhere and that you are an eternal part of it all.

Know that angels are with you.

You are within love.

You are within light.

You are therefore within abundance.

Always.

Forever.

Be within that everlasting feeling and let it fill all of you. Stop reading this book when you feel yourself securely protected by the power of love, light, and angels. You are part of it all. You are part of limitless love and light, and nothing can limit the limitless.

Move further into your childhood and lovingly look around. Do you feel there is something else that is important? Do you see some more moments that you can fill with light and love? Close your eyes and feel. Take your time. You don't have to seek those moments because they will find their way to you. They have waited a long time to meet you, and they are grateful that you are immersing them in light and love. Do it. Do it now, and everything becomes love.

Childhood is a set of memories that you carry along your journey in this world. Fill those memories with love and light. Ask the all-powerful angels, God's messengers, to travel with you and to go forward with courage. You will be accompanied by a choir of angels, in the strength of light and with love in your heart. Traveling in this way, you will discover beautiful feelings within yourself and marvelous experiences in front of you. Spread love all around you, and the power of love will never desert you.

Accept this everywhere within you.

This is you.

The power of light and the bearer of light.

Acknowledge all of this.

Feel how God is doing the same beside you.

You are together with God.

You are together with angels.

You are holy.

You are angelic.

I see you becoming marvelously bright. You are so precious to the world. The whole world thanks you. It is the ultimate gift to the world when you present love to it with this marvelous light. The world will not forget you; therefore, you are one with the world. You may now live in this world with a peaceful heart. Now you may continue your journey through life with absolute peace and love in your heart.

Go bravely onward with a childlike honesty because your memories contain love, which creates abundance around you and within you. You stopped before a small rock and started to think about whether you should step over it or go around it. Look carefully at that rock. That rock is your feelings and thoughts that arise when you hear the words "journey through life." You don't need to step over or go around it. You no longer have to fear your journey through life.

Bravely lift that rock up. Look at how small that rock has become. You recall how you struggled to carry that heavy burden on your back along life's path. Now that rock has become small and lovely. You have released so many burdens that you were carrying through life. Only this small rock full of feelings and thoughts of life's journey has remained.

You looked forward and tried to understand the course of your life's journey. You saw a twisting path that led into the distance and out of sight. At that, you were filled with insecurity. You couldn't see where the path would lead. The limits that tied you to your past lives dug a small hollow into your body of light. The path led somewhere, but you didn't know where. You were a traveler on that twisting path, and everyone had to carry his or her own rock on it—so says human experience from your past lives.

Shake your whole body and throw off the thought that has held you to your past notions of life's journey. You are not a rock on the side of the road, and you don't need to fear a kick from every passerby. You are not carrying a rock on an unknown journey through life. You don't have to fear rocks that may appear on your journey.

You carry light.

You are light.

Look again at the rock you have picked up and send it love. Do you see it? That stone has already become quite small, and now, you can create a miracle.

You are light.

You inhale light, and when you exhale, everything changes to light around you.

Inhale the beloved light. Lift that rock, which yearns for love, to your mouth and breathe light on it. Breathe the light that comes from within and admire the rock in your hand. A miracle happens. It is only a miracle for humans because this is a natural movement for the universe. The rock changes into pure gold in your hand.

Continue to breathe your almighty light on it, and you can see how that the piece of gold transforms into golden light and starts to float above your hands. You see a miraculous golden sphere glowing in front of you. You look at it and can't take your eyes away from it. This is your creation. You are a creator.

You are light, and you create light.

That miraculous sphere of light gently floats nearer, and instantly you notice that a small hollow has appeared in your body of light due to your doubtful thoughts. You are astonished at how perfectly the sphere of light, which you have created, fits into that hollow and as if on purpose. The sphere of light completely fills the hollow place. In the next moment, you sense that the sphere has merged into your body of light. You are whole again. You have made yourself whole. You are a healer, yes you are—the healer of yourself and world. Yes you! As all other healers working together, uniting their spiritual power and knowledge.

Everything is love.

Healing is reaching into love and being within love.

Being is love.

Breathe in love and feel how your body of light turns more radiant. Breathe out love and see how the light around you becomes more radiant. Look around, and you no longer see the twisting path of life leading into the unknown. Everything around you has become light, and you don't have to wander. Your journey through life has become your journey of being. The whole journey has become being in golden light here and now.

Breathe in love, and you receive the most important gift in this world from which everything is born. Breathe in love, and you are in the light that dissolves all the limits of being. That gives you release. That gives you unlimited freedom to travel effortlessly with the power of love between the past, present, and future, as time and its forms are known to this world.

Accept this freedom. Race into the past at lightning speed and experience it with a childish joy and without any fear. Radiate light on everything. When you get tired of that, change direction and with enthusiasm and joy, sprint at lightning speed toward the future. Sparkle in the light. Laugh with happiness and be thrilled with everything that you experience.

You are of light. Cast light everywhere around you, wherever you may be. This is a wonderful moment. Enjoy it. Enjoy it everywhere. Send love everywhere and be in light everywhere. This is real freedom. You are born free because you are born of light. You are free with light. Freedom brings joy into life, and joy in life radiates into love.

Breathe in the joy of life.

Breathe in love. You are free.

You are in light.

You are.

As a human being, you find yourself in the playground of your experiences on this earth. This chapter in your life is a wonderful gift for you to experience. You create your experiences and yourself, and through this, you create the whole world. Your own world is an irreplaceable and unique little piece in the puzzle of the whole world. Your creation is vital to the whole world. The world thanks you for it. The angels thank you because they are always with you. We are all together as one whole.

Sooner or later, as people say, in a heavenly moment, you arrive in a beautiful garden full of abundance and love, and your heart draws you toward an apple tree in the middle of it.

You pray God for sobriety so that you can experience with all your senses the exquisite beauty around you and of everything that is. You gently touch the bark of the apple tree, admire the tree's thick canopy, and run your hands along the hanging branches. You admire the beautiful apples that the tree has created in gratitude of the Creator.

You are fortunate. Your heart sings. Your soul bursts with happiness. You are grateful to God. You are grateful to the world that has given you the opportunity to be here and now. You feel the exquisite sound of light in your ears. You really hear it. It is truly wonderful.

Everything is light, and everything is love. Suddenly, you listen. You recognize the tintinnabulation of light, which is in harmony with your light. In this garden of abundance, the sound is so familiar and close. It comes nearer. Your heart beats rapidly with recognition. You have sought and waited for that sound. You have prayed to hear that sound. Now you hear it at last, right here.

The same sound of light, which rings in you, comes closer. A wonderful light floats toward you through the garden of abundance. It is a loving and precious light. You recognize it. The sound of that light unites beautifully with the sound of your light. Your sound is its sound, and its sound is your sound. God blesses that moment of reunion and angels sing a prayer of thanks.

You notice how the wonderful light that floats closer to you emits for a brief moment different symbols that remind you of something very important. They are signals that you have been waiting for. You have waited and have searched for them throughout your lives. You respond with your own symbols embracing the one who has sought and waited for you through many lives. You recognize each other. You are two parts of one whole, soulmates. You have finally found each other.

You were born as twin lights from the source of light. At one time, you shared a delicious apple under the apple tree. You set out on life's journey together. God gave you His blessing, which you forgot during your past lives and you even started to doubt its existence. Only occasionally, you have remembered this meeting by the tree of the knowledge of good and evil as human experience has called it. Every image of life you encountered has been created by you because you are a creator. As a human being, you have forgotten this over time. But the sound of light is unforgettable. The memory of light cannot be extinguished. The sound of light remains forever. You have just realized this.

Now you hear only this sound—the unison of light. You sleep and awake in this, time after time, because nothing else can draw you in except that marvelous recognition.

You have found each other again, eternal soulmates. You come closer to each other, and the harmony within you becomes more intense and enchanting. Your bodies of light tenderly touch each other, and the sparkling alertness created by that touch makes you take a deep breath of love and light. You are together again.

As you are together, you suddenly notice all the signs which helped you recognize each other through different lifetimes. Yes, those were from you. Now you can affirm all those

longed-for meetings from life to life get affirmed. Yes, you have searched for each other and have found each other. You notice how your tears of joy at meeting once more turn into golden drops. You gather them tenderly and offer them to each other as a gift from your journey into this human world. Your bodies of light merge into one marvelous golden light. Listen to the sound of your light. It can be heard throughout the universe, and it sends love—your endless love—because you were born of love, and love is your real home. You have become one again. We are one. We are love. We are light.

Love, light, love, light, love, light

We are love. Trust love.

About the Author

Martin Napa was born in Tallinn, Estonia. After graduating from the university he became a lawyer. He has worked as a diplomat, as well as a counselor to different national ministers and international public and private limited companies. He has also studied theology and different cultures around the world. Photography has been his long-standing hobby and he enjoys immensely sea, sailing to islands near and far. His true calling since childhood has been to become a writer.

His first novel, *The Message to Egypt*, which was written under the pseudonym Martin Paan, appeared in 1998. In 2003, this was followed by his next novel, *Creation*. In 2006, *Formula for Living* appeared in the essay genre. In 2008, *Angel's Diary* was first published in the Estonian language. His book of poems, *The Spot of Light*, appeared in 2016.

Angels touched Martin's heart in 2003 when he had an opportunity to take part in angel therapy courses in Ireland together with his wife, Mai-Liis. She is also an illustrator of *Angel's Diary*.

Author didn't know then about the difficulties ahead, but the presence of God's angels has made it possible to endure the challenging times and sorrow. Angels love us without judging us, in light as in darkness, because their ultimate wish is to help and guide us to the understanding that we are one whole. That we deserve forgiveness as we should forgive everyone else. We are love. Only love is everlasting. Angels strive to pass this on to all humans. This message only needs to be recognized, put into words, and passed on.